HISTORIC

COMMUNITIES

The Victorian Home

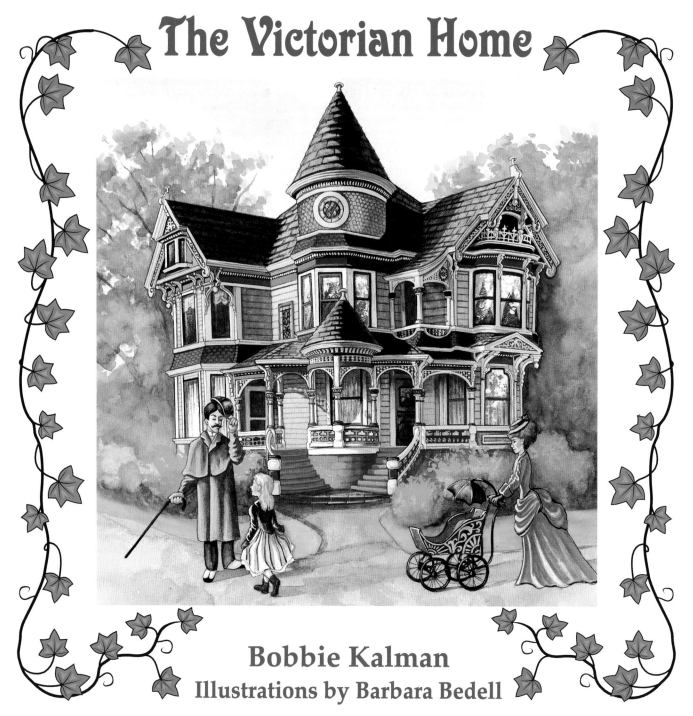

Bobbie Kalman

Illustrations by Barbara Bedell

Crabtree Publishing Company

www.crabtreebooks.com

HISTORIC
COMMUNITIES

Created by Bobbie Kalman

For Barbara Bedell, whose wonderful
artwork brings our books to life

Editor-in-Chief
Bobbie Kalman

Research
April Fast
Hannelore Sotzek

Writing team
Bobbie Kalman
April Fast

Managing editor
Lynda Hale

Editors
Niki Walker
Greg Nickles
Petrina Gentile

Computer design
Lynda Hale

Special thanks to
The Preservation Gallery (cover); Biltmore Estate; Kenneth
Heaman and Montgomery's Inn; Molly Brown House Museum;
James Whitcomb Riley Memorial Association; Carol Wells and
Saratoga Springs Preservation Foundation; Naumkeag and
The Trustees of Reservations; Jamie Maxwell and The Toronto
Historical Board; The Grand Victorian; U.S. Grant Home State
Historic Site and The Illinois Historic Preservation Agency;
U.S.D.I. National Park Service; John Muir National Historic Site;
The Harriet Beecher Stowe Center; President Benjamin Harrison
Home; Strawbery Banke

All illustrations by Barbara Bedell except the following:
Janet Kimantas: pages 1, 11
Patrick Ingoldsby: page 22

Separations and film
Dot 'n Line Image Inc.

Printer
Worzalla Publishing Company

Crabtree Publishing Company

PMB 16A
350 Fifth Ave.,
Suite 3308
N.Y., N.Y. 10118

612 Welland Ave.,
St. Catharines,
Ontario, Canada
L2M 5V6

73 Lime Walk
Headington
Oxford OX3 7AD
United Kingdom

Cataloging in Publication Data
Kalman, Bobbie, 1947-
  The Victorian home

(Historic communities series)
Includes index.
ISBN 0-86505-431-2 (library bound) ISBN 0-86505-461-4 (pbk.)
This book examines the exteriors, interiors, and furnishings
of Victorian-style homes.

1. Dwellings - United States - Juvenile literature. 2. United States -
Social life and customs - 19th century - Juvenile literature.
3. Dwellings - Canada - Juvenile literature. 4. Canada - Social life
and customs - 19th century - Juvenile literature. I. Bedell, Barbara.
II. Title. III. Series: Kalman, Bobbie, 1947-   . Historic communities.

GT228.K3 1996   j392.36'00971   LC 96-26733
                                                         CIP

Contents

The Victorian era

The Victorian era was the period of time between 1837 and 1901, when Queen Victoria ruled Britain. In North America, these were years of growth and change. Factories opened, and people moved to the cities to find jobs or start businesses. Some earned a lot of money and built large, fancy homes.

Not all Victorian homes were large, but even the smaller ones were decorated carefully. People wanted to create a home that was an inviting, comfortable retreat from the busy world outside.

Fancy, but cosy

The rooms in which guests were entertained were designed with great detail. Walls were covered with richly patterned wallpaper and adorned with pictures and mirrors. Tables and shelves were covered with lace cloths and cluttered with flower arrangements, treasured knickknacks, and pictures. Even ceilings were ornamented with paint, wallpaper, or drapery.

Changing tastes

For much of the Victorian period, furniture was made of dark, heavy, intricately carved wood. Couches and chairs were upholstered in luxurious fabrics such as velvet and brocade. Near the end of the nineteenth century, people grew tired of the dark colors and cluttered rooms. They took down the heavy drapes and put up light and airy curtains. They replaced the dark furniture with chairs, tables, and cabinets made of light-colored wood. Rooms also had less furniture and fewer knickknacks.

Victorian decorators loved to drape fabrics over windows, beds, tables, and fireplace mantels. In this room, even the ceiling is draped.

opposite page (top) Dining-room tables, chairs, and buffets were often made of walnut or mahogany.
(bottom left) The canopy bed was popular during the early part of the Victorian era.
(bottom right) The furniture in most Victorian sitting rooms was arranged in small, cosy groupings to allow people to chat.

On the outside

There were several styles of Victorian homes. Most were two or three stories high. Some had front porches with carved wooden railings and spindles. Painted shutters sometimes adorned the windows. When most people think of a Victorian home, they think of the Queen Anne style. Some Queen Anne homes had stained-glass windows. Peaks, towers, bay windows, and wraparound porches were part of the Queen Anne design.

Some Queen Anne homes were known as "painted ladies." Ornate woodwork, called **gingerbread trim,** *decorated the porches and gables. People used at least three colors of paint on the house exterior, pillars, and trim.*

Victorian homes were made of brick, clapboard, and stone. A variety of shapes was used in designing each home. Place some tracing paper over the houses on these two pages and trace as many shapes as you can see. How many triangles have you found? Don't forget the squares, circles, rectangles, ovals, domes, cylinders, and hexagons! Design your own Victorian home using as many shapes as you can. Add pillars, porches, and gingerbread trim.

Come into the parlor

The most formal room in a Victorian house was the **parlor**. It was also called the **salon** or **drawing room** and was used only for Sunday family gatherings and entertaining guests. The parlor was located at the front of the house near the entrance hall. After a guest was greeted, or **received**, in the hallway, he or she was invited into the parlor.

A dark, private room

Most parlors were decorated in deep, rich colors such as burgundy or dark green. Windows were covered with layers of heavy drapes to keep sunlight from fading the rugs, furniture, and wallpaper. Stained-glass windows also filtered out the sun and made the room private and cosy. During chilly weather, a fire warmed the parlor.

Little room to move

The parlor contained a lot of furniture to show off the family's wealth and good taste. A painted or embroidered fire screen stood before the fireplace to stop shooting sparks. The screen also kept heat away from those sitting close to the fire. The many chairs, tables, footstools, and small couches, called **settees**, left little floor space.

Always a fresh seat

The parlor was crowded with chairs, not just for show, but also for the sake of good manners. When a woman entered a room, it was considered rude for a man to offer her his seat because the cushion might still be warm. The parlor was cluttered with chairs to ensure there would always be a fresh seat.

The Victorian kitchen

Early Victorian kitchens were located in the basement because people wanted to keep food odors and grease away from the rest of the house. In later Victorian homes, the kitchen was on the first floor.

Kitchen tables

The most important item in the kitchen was a large, sturdy table. Its legs were painted, but its top was left natural so that the wooden surface could be scrubbed daily. There were also smaller tables for chopping food, drying dishes, and rolling pastry. A **dough box** was a table with a removable box or trough. Bread dough was kneaded on the tabletop, put into the box, and then placed near the warm stove to help it rise.

Bugs were a problem in the kitchen. To help control insects, many people kept a hedgehog in the basement. It curled up and slept during the day but roamed around the dark kitchen at night, eating cockroaches and other insects.

Stoves and fireplaces for cooking

Early Victorian kitchens had a large fireplace, but later homes had one or more stoves. Stoves were better than fireplaces for both cooking and heating. The heat from a stove stayed in the room instead of escaping up the chimney, as it did in a fireplace. As an added convenience, many stoves also had built-in water heaters and bake ovens.

Storing food, dishes, and candles

Dishes and groceries were stored in tall wooden cabinets with glass doors that kept the shelves free of dust. **Safes** or **tin closets** were cabinets with screens or pierced-tin windows in their doors to keep bugs and other pests away from food. Pies were stored in a small cabinet called a **pie safe**. Candles were kept in tin tubes to prevent mice from nibbling them.

Find the following kitchen items in the picture below:

1. *chopping/pastry table*
2. *trencher*
3. *butcher's block*
4. *water pump*
5. *dry sink*
6. *pie safe*
7. *ice cabinet*
8. *punched-tin candle tube*
9. *weigh scale*
10. *coffee grinder*

Answers:

1-D; 2-H, 3-I; 4-C; 5-J; 6-G; 7-A; 8-E; 9-B; 10-F

Servants in the home

Many families hired servants to help with the cooking and cleaning. Some servants lived in the house and slept in rooms called the servants' **quarters**. The quarters were usually on the top floor of the house or in the basement, where the servants did much of their work. The rooms were small and dark and had only a bed and a dresser. The owners of the home did not bother to make their servants' bedrooms and workrooms cheerful or comfortable.

The food pantry

Keeping the **food pantry** stocked was just one of the servants' many jobs. The food pantry was a large closet in the basement that stored supplies of **staples**. Staples are foods that do not spoil quickly, so they can be kept in large quantities for a long time. Jars of pickles, jams, and vegetables and tins of coffee, tea, and sugar were some of the items found in the pantry.

Working in the scullery

Servants washed dishes and polished silver and brass in the **scullery**. This workroom was also used as a storeroom for household items such as brooms, feather dusters, washtubs and washboards, and other cleaning supplies.

Sometimes a stove was located in the scullery as well as in the kitchen. Victorian homes did not have hot running water, so when the kitchen stove was being used for cooking, the scullery stove heated water for filling bathtubs and washing dishes. Laundry was also boiled on the scullery stove.

*A **call box** in the basement signaled when a servant was needed upstairs. To call a servant, a person pulled a knob or sash that was connected to the call box. A bell rang, and a number popped up in the box. The number told the servant which room was calling.*

The dining room

The dining room was often the scene of lavish dinner parties. In order to impress guests, the hosts draped the table with fine linens or lace and set it using their best china, silverware, and crystal.

In early Victorian homes, the dining room was located in the basement, near the kitchen. People thought that food was digested better in the dark, so the basement was considered the best spot in which to eat. Later on, the dining room was moved upstairs to the main floor. This formal room was used only for dinner. Breakfast and lunch were eaten in the kitchen.

Summer and winter curtains

In summer, curtains made of light material were hung on the windows. Wooden blinds also shaded the room from sunlight. In winter, heavy drapes were put up to keep heat in the house. People found, however, that the thick material trapped unpleasant odors. In later years, lighter curtains were left up year round.

Dining room furniture

The furniture was dark and heavy. The large table could seat several people, especially when **leaves**, or extra pieces, were added to it. When the table was not in use, it was covered with a tablecloth. The massive, carved **sideboard**, or china cabinet, displayed fancy porcelain dishes, crystal, and silver. A **buffet**, which resembled a long dresser, provided extra storage space. A **tea cart** or **dinner wagon** was used to wheel food and drinks to the table.

The dumbwaiter

When the kitchen was still in the basement and the dining room was upstairs, food had to be carried quite a distance before it reached the table. A **dumbwaiter** transported meals quickly and easily. A dumbwaiter is a shelf that moves up and down a long tunnel or chute. Using a system of ropes and pulleys, a servant hoisted dinner up to the dining room. It was then placed on the dinner wagon and served at the table. The dirty dishes were later returned to the kitchen on the dumbwaiter.

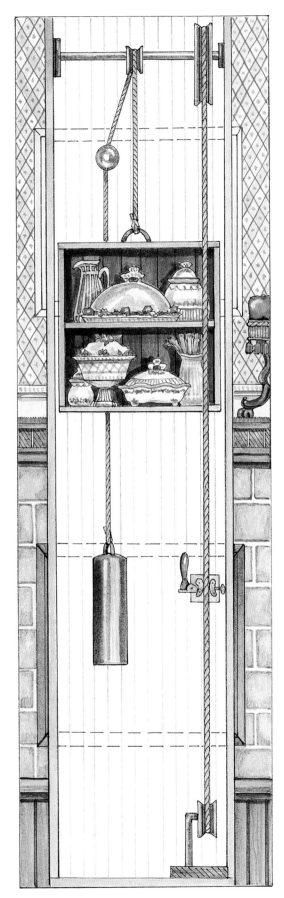

The dumbwaiter saved servants a great deal of walking. It also allowed them to serve food hot because they could move dinner from the stove to the table in much less time.

Bed chambers

Bedrooms, or **bed chambers**, were considered very private. They were located on the second floor and were never viewed by visitors—even a glimpse was considered improper!

A place for relaxing

Unlike earlier bedrooms, Victorian bed chambers were used for reading, sewing, and relaxing, as well as for sleeping. Chairs, tables, and settees were snugly arranged around the fireplace.

No closets

Victorian bedrooms did not have closets. Instead, clothes were stored in chests of drawers, or **bureaus**. Skirts, dresses, and suits were hung in tall cabinets with doors, called **wardrobes**.

Big beds

Beds were large and fancy. Bed frames were made of elaborately carved wood or curved brass or iron. Mattresses were stuffed with goose feathers, straw, or horsehair.

A popular Victorian bed was the **four-poster**, named for the tall posts that rose toward the ceiling from each corner of the bed. Sometimes the tops of the posts were connected by a wooden frame. The frame was covered with fabric, making a **canopy**. For added warmth and privacy, curtains were hung from the frame.

Washing in the bedrooms

Early Victorian homes did not have running water or bathrooms, but every bedroom had a **washstand**. A washstand stood waist-high and had two shelves.

The top shelf had a hole in which a basin and pitcher rested. The lower shelf, sometimes hidden behind cabinet doors, held the **commode set**. The commode set included a soap dish, toothbrush, cup, and shaving mug.

Chamber pots

When it was too cold to go to the outhouse, **chamber pots** were used for nighttime emergencies. Each room had one hidden in a chair or under the bed. Servants emptied the pots each morning.

The water closet

In the first part of the nineteenth century, people considered bathing to be a lot of trouble. In order to take a hot bath, they had to heat water on a stove in the basement and carry it all the way upstairs to the bedroom.

Indoor plumbing was available during the Victorian era, but it was very expensive. Those who could afford it, converted unused bedrooms into bathrooms, or **water closets**. Water closets had fireplaces, stained-glass windows, richly papered walls, and hardwood floors.

Hidden sinks, tubs, and toilets

People were shy about having water closets, so they disguised sinks, faucets, and pipes as dressers. Tubs were enclosed in wooden boxes that resembled large chests or cabinets. People went to great lengths to hide toilets from view. In some homes, the toilet was behind a curtain or screen. In others, it was in a room of its own.

Later bathrooms

In the late 1800s, water closets began to look more like the bathrooms of today. People became less shy about having them. Sinks and toilets were no longer disguised as furniture or hidden behind privacy screens. Claw-footed tubs replaced boxed-in tubs.

A place for children

Children spent most of their time in the nursery. The nursery was either a single room or a group of rooms where children ate, played, studied, and slept. It was often located away from the bedrooms of the adults because parents did not want to be disturbed by their children.

Plain, simple, and clean

Most nurseries were plain and had simple furniture. Walls were often painted so they could be scrubbed clean. Sometimes the walls were covered with painted tiles or murals that showed fairy tales and nursery rhymes. Instead of wall-to-wall carpeting, children's rooms had wooden floors with small area rugs that could be removed when children were playing.

During the day, children did not spend much time with their mothers and fathers. Parents made a special trip to the nursery to see them in the evening. The visits lasted about an hour.

Sweet dreams for baby

Safety was an important factor in choosing a child's bed. Rocking cradles were considered unsafe, so most babies slept in cribs. Cribs were made of wood, wicker, or iron. Some children slept on a cot with high wooden sides that kept them from falling out during the night.

Beds for older children

Older children slept in a **rope bed**, which had ropes strung across the wooden frame to support the mattress. **Trundle beds** were common in nurseries that housed more than one child. During the day, the low, lightweight trundle bed was pushed underneath a higher one, giving the children more room to play.

*Many children were taught in a schoolroom that was part of the nursery. Some had a private teacher, or **governess**, and others were given basic lessons by their nanny.*

Heating and lighting the home

Fire screens often had colorful flowers and designs painted or embroidered on the side that faced the room.

Victorian homes did not have electricity or central heating. Most rooms were lit by candles and gas or oil lamps. They were heated by fireplaces or wood-burning stoves.

The essential fireplace

Fireplaces were the main source of heat and light, and they also made rooms look attractive. Family pictures, clocks, vases, and other knickknacks were displayed on the carved mantel. A fire screen stood guard in front of the fire.

Bed warmers

Not all bedrooms had fireplaces, so beds were often chilly in winter. Before climbing into bed, people heated their sheets and blankets with a bed warmer. A bed warmer was a metal container with a long wooden handle. The container was filled with hot coals. Heat from the coals escaped through holes in its lid. People held the handle and slid the container around under the blankets.

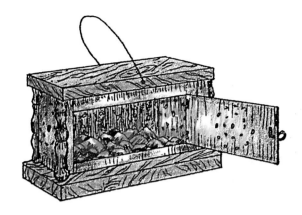

Foot warmers were filled with hot coals. People placed their feet near them to keep their toes warm.

Sconces and chandeliers

In early Victorian homes, candles provided light for reading and other evening activities. **Sconces** made candlelight brighter by reflecting it into the room. Sconces were made of tin, brass, or silver that was polished to a shiny finish. They were placed on tables or attached to walls. **Chandeliers** were large candleholders that hung from the ceiling.

Bed warmers had to be moved around quickly so they would not burn the sheets.

Oil and kerosene lamps

The first oil lamps burned fish oil or grease. Although they burned longer than candles did, the smoke from the oil was dirty and smelly, and the light was not very bright. Many people preferred using candles, even though making them was a messy job.

By the mid-1800s, **kerosene** became available as a fuel for lamps. Kerosene was clean, inexpensive, and burned for a long time. Natural gas was more expensive and was used mainly in the homes of the wealthy. **Gasoliers** were magnificent hanging lamps fueled by natural gas. By the end of the century, electricity became available in cities, and many homeowners converted their gasoliers and chandeliers to electric lights.

This old chandelier used to hold candles, but now it is lit with bulbs that resemble candle flames.

Items found in the home

In the Victorian era, people had more money to spend on their homes than they did in the years before. Beautiful decorations and nifty household gadgets became especially popular as people tried to make their home relaxing and comfortable. Although many objects were simply used for decoration, some were designed cleverly to hide things that were considered embarrassing or unattractive.

*In some homes, the basin, pitcher, and commode set were stored in a **commode chest**. People were embarrassed about cleaning their bodies, so they kept their washing utensils out of sight under the lid of the chest. A **slop jar** holding dirty wash water was hidden behind the door.*

Hair work *or* **hair art** *was popular. Women made pictures, wreaths, and bouquets from their own hair or the hair of a family member. The art was framed and displayed in the parlor. Sometimes it was given to loved ones as a token of affection because it contained a part of the giver.*

*A **spittoon** or **cuspidor** was a spit bowl used to catch tobacco juice. Some spittoons were hidden in the drawer of a special smoker's chair. Other spittoons were disguised as a vase.*

*Once people had indoor plumbing, they enjoyed warm baths regularly. Soon, gadgets were invented for the bathtub. One such gadget was the **shower bath ring**. It fit over a person's head and rested on the shoulders. A hose connected the ring to the faucet. Water sprayed from holes in the bottom of the ring and flowed over the entire body without wetting hair, walls, or floors.*

Some rocking chairs were designed to disguise a chamber pot. People had to be careful not to rock too quickly!

*A lot of men used **macassar oil** to slick back their hair. Crocheted doilies, called **anti-macassars**, were put over the backs of chairs to keep this grease from staining the furniture.*

Mansions of the wealthy

Some Victorian homes were so big that they were called **mansions**. Mansions had several special-purpose rooms that were not often found in smaller homes. They also had magnificent gardens with fountains and statues.

Library

Collecting books was an expensive hobby because most books were bound in leather and imported from Europe. Some mansion owners had a library to house their large collection of books. The walls of the library were lined with rows of bookshelves. In some libraries, the shelves were behind glass doors to keep dust away from the books. In others, curtains were hung on brass rods to protect the books.

Many Victorian mansions were built to look like European castles. This mansion in North Carolina resembles a French château.

(opposite page) This library was designed for both reading and daydreaming. If a person was not in the mood to read, he or she could stare at the beautiful ceiling.

Ballroom

Ballrooms were found only in the grandest of homes. They were large open rooms that were lavishly decorated with chandeliers, mirrors, flowers, and plants. Grand balls and other large gatherings were held in the ballroom. Music for dancing was provided by a small orchestra.

The smoking room

The smoking room was the only room in which men could smoke without offending the women of the house. In those days, women were not allowed to smoke. Having a separate smoking room also kept the smelly smoke from being absorbed by the furniture or drapes in other rooms. Men protected their clothing and hair from smoke by wearing special jackets and velvet caps. Smoking rooms were also found in smaller homes.

Large Victorian homes often had a billiard room. The game of billiards was popular in the nineteenth century.

Music room

Music was a popular form of entertainment in the Victorian era. Many homes had musical instruments in their parlors, but mansions often had a room devoted to music. Love seats, chairs, tea tables, and cushions were arranged around beautiful instruments such as a piano and harp. After dinner, family and guests enjoyed musical performances that included singing.

Conservatory

People who were interested in flowers had a **conservatory** on the main floor of their mansion. A conservatory was a greenhouse decorated with plant stands, wicker furniture, and cast-iron fountains and garden sets. Rock gardens and caged songbirds were added to increase the feeling of being outdoors.

Many mansions had vast yards that looked like parks. This conservatory is not part of the house but is a separate building surrounded by gardens.

Victorian ways

In the Victorian era, men and women had very different roles. The man was the head of the household and was expected to support his wife and children. It was the wife's duty to make a pleasant, comfortable home for her family. In front of others, she was well dressed and behaved in a prim, proper manner. People believed that a wife's behavior reflected on her husband. In the photograph above, women are socializing in the parlor after a dinner party. Where are the men?

After a dinner party, men retired to the library or smoking room to talk to one another. If there was a billiard room, the men went there to play pool. The parlor was considered the "women's room."

Many people wanted to impress others with their possessions. Find different items above that were used to make this parlor look rich. Which items would you remove or change if you were an interior decorator?

Glossary

bay window A window that projects from a wall of a building

canopy A covering that is supported over a bed by four posts

cast-iron A hard type of iron

central heating A system of heating many rooms from one main source

chamber pot A metal or ceramic pot used in place of a toilet or outhouse

chandelier A fancy light fixture that hangs from the ceiling

clapboard Wooden siding on a house

claw-footed bathtub A raised bathtub with feet that resemble a bird's talons or a lion's claws

commode set A set containing a soap dish, toothbrush, cup, and shaving mug

crocheted Describing needlework that resembles knitting but requires only one needle

dinner wagon A cart used to transport meals to the table

embroidered Describing something that has been decorated with needlework

feather duster A clump of feathers attached to a handle and used for dusting

fringe A decorative trim of hanging threads or cords

gable A triangular feature of a building, used as decoration over a door or window

gingerbread trim Ornate wooden trim on the edge of porches or roofs

indoor plumbing A system of pipes that carries water into and out of a building

kerosene A type of fuel burned in lamps

knickknack A small, decorative object

leaf A piece of wood that is added to a tabletop to make it longer

mahogany A tree with hard, reddish-brown wood

mansion A very large house with many rooms

mural A picture or scene painted on a wall or ceiling

ornate Describing something that is detailed or elaborate

porcelain A type of fine ceramic

settee A small sofa

spindle A long, slender post used to support a railing

trencher A wooden bowl made from a hollowed-out log, used to mix and serve food

upholstered Describing furniture that has stuffing, springs, and cushions and is covered with fabric

Victorian Describing the period of time between 1837 and 1901, when Queen Victoria ruled Britain; describing objects, styles, or people of this time

walnut A tree with hard, dark wood

washboard A board used for washing laundry by scrubbing it against metal or glass ridges

washstand A cabinet or table used to hold a pitcher and basin

wicker Thin twigs that are braided and woven together to make furniture

wraparound porch A porch or verandah that extends around one or more corners of a house

31

Index

Acknowledgments

Photographs and reproductions
Courtesy of Biltmore Estate, Asheville,
    North Carolina: pages 4, 5 (both bottom),
    26, 27, 28, 29
Marc Crabtree: page 10
Lynda Hale: cover
Bobbie Kalman: pages 6, 7 (both bottom), 23
Reuters/Archive Photos: page 30
Saratoga Springs Preservation Foundation:
    page 7 (top, middle)
Spadina House/Toronto Historical Board:
    pages 5 (top), 22
The Mark Twain House, Hartford, CT:
    pages 14, 20, 21

About the homes
The **Preservation Gallery** (cover and page 6) was
built in 1886 for the granddaughter of a former
slave. Today, this Queen-Anne Victorian is a fine-
art gallery in Niagara-on-the-Lake, Ontario.
The **Biltmore House** (pages 4, 5 both bottom,
26-29) in Asheville, North Carolina, was George
Washington Vanderbilt's country home. Built in
1895, it is a French Renaissance-styled mansion.
The **Mark Twain House** (pages 14, 20, 21) in
Hartford, Connecticut, is a Victorian Gothic
mansion completed in 1874 and owned by author
Mark Twain until 1903. **Spadina House** (pages 5
top, 22) in Toronto, Ontario, is a mid-Victorian
country home built by James Austin in 1866.

5 6 7 8 9 0   Printed in the U.S.A.   5 4 3 2